Love the Sinner
Hate the Cinema
Poison Capsule Reviews

I0170195

E. Basil St. Blaise

Illustrated by
Randy Jones
&
Martin Kozlowski

Front cover by Martin Kozlowski
Illustrations by Randy Jones
& Martin Kozlowski
Edited by Martin Kozlowski

For more Critic's Corner reviews,
please visit nowwhatmedia.com

For more on Now What Media Books,
please visit nowwhatmedia.com/nowwhatbooks.html

E. Basil St. Blaise

A St. Blaise of Glory

Stated simply, for E. Basil St. Blaise, the noted author and critic, life is art and entertainment, and art and entertainment is…are life. E. Basil grew up with his doting father, Basil E., and a surrogate mother he knew only as Estrellita in a small Midwestern town some years before the first remake of a *A Star is Born*. His earliest memories are of freshly-baked dingleberry pies, Uncle Miltie on the RCA television, Uncle Stu on Estrellita and amateur theatre at the famed Hogshead Abattoir (where they routinely butchered Williams, Odets and Genet.) He read everything he could get his hands on, usually before it was hung in the privy, and he spent countless nights nestled under the covers with his flashlight and a jar of Estrellita's cold cream.

E. Basil St. Blaise and his faithful four-legged companion, Josef

After graduating in the top fifty of his admittedly small high school class at Roscoe Arbuckle Memorial he fulfilled his life-long fantasy of coming to New York to attend the John Derek Junior College for the Performing Arts. Though he stayed for just one all-too-brief semester before a civil suit forced the institution to shutter its doors, he absorbed all the sights, sounds and putrefactive smells that Broadway and the Big City had to offer. It was for the school newspaper, *Thespian Tendencies,* which he penned his first bylined review of an Off Broadway production of *Waiting for Godot* performed in Tagalog. His brief comment ("I hope these waiters kept their job at Horn & Hardart.") published under the heading *Kritic's Korner* was a hit with readers. Sadly, his editor let him go for failing to fill his allotted 6-inch column space.

Upon his return to the "sticks" St. Blaise began honing his "short, but sour" reviews in a wide range of publications including Penny Savers, church newsletters, and public health pamphlets. He critiqued everything from local art exhibitions ("This Sunday painter should follow the Lord's example and rest on the seventh day.") to state fair beauty pageants ("As Charlotte wrote in her web: SOME PIG.") to quilting bees ("May they dip their needles in curare.") to barber shop quartets ("Where's a straight razor when you need one?") A double-bill at the local Bijou of *Rashomon* and *The Amazing Colossal Man* proved to be a revelation to the budding critic and he vowed from that day forth to "Love the sinner, hate the cinema."

He clawed his way through the journalistic jungle with a steady stream of submissions to many of the most prestigious publications of the 1970s, appearing only occasionally in their letters columns under a string of assumed noms de pan. His scathing potshots at other critics' darlings like *The Godfather* ("Do Wops."), *Bonnie and Clyde* ("Should be Dunaway with."), *Nashville* ("He whore."), *A Clockwork Orange* ("Kubrick-a-brack."), and *The French Connection* ("The dope's in the director's chair.") did catch the attention of the editors of *Cinema Nihilisme* in France who began reproducing his denunciations.

As fate would have it, the July, 1976 edition was purchased by both Henri Langlois, France's greatest cinéaste and founder of the Musée du Cinema and Pauline Kael, the New Yorker's preeminent critic of the day. St. Blaise's two-word review of the newly-released *Taxi Driver* ("Hack job.") was printed in English on page 84. Langlois did not understand it and Kael's copy was missing pages 82 through 86 due to a printer's error.

St. Blaise's New Trails

In 1962 a precocious St. Blaise helped establish the adult film industry's first award for excellence, the Wanky, and was there in the back row of the New Adonis Theatre in New York's Times Square for its inaugural presentation. The Gland Prize winner that year was the infamous *Long Day's Journey into Mike* accepted by its star Lash Lagroine. The Palme D'Whore for best peep show went to *The Longest Lay* (which, ironically, took 96 quarters to view in its entirety.)

He has been guest lecturer at the Earl Dittman Correspondence School for Constructive Criticism since 2002. As a film programmer he has organized the Fire Island Selected Shorts Festival, the Crawford, Texas Barking Spider Comedy Jamboree, and the Surveillance Tape Bloopers Fest in Langley, Virginia. He has been consulted on assembling the action film video library of North Korea's Kim Jong-il and a Whitney Huston DVD collection for a reclusive collector in Abbottabad, Pakistan.

He is the author of numerous books on the cinematic arts including *Your Sleeve's Too Short to Box with God* on the history of bad costume design and *The Camera's Bleary Eye*, a history of focus pullers with macular degeneration. He has ghost written several unauthorized showbiz biographies including *Loni: MILF No More* and *Haley Joel: After the Lollipops*. He is currently working on a roman á clef concerning a big star with a drinking problem whose arrest and various anti-Semitic tirades threaten to ruin his career, tentatively entitled *You'll Never Eat Lox in This Town Again*.

He has dispensed his buttery pop scorn online in the Critic's Corner at nowwhatmedia.com since 2007. The reviews in this volume have been culled from the best burnt offerings of the past five years.

—Martin Kozlowski

The Illustrators

Randy Jones

Randy Jones was born on a potato farm in Exeter, Ontario, Canada, and he's been drawing pictures since he was a small fry. He was influenced by Koko the Clown cartoons on early television, and by any movie with cowboys and indians, gladiators, pirates, Tarzan, or the Ten Commandments.

His artwork has appeared in many major publications including the *Wall Street Journal*, the *New York Times*, *Playboy*, *Newsday*, and the *National Lampoon*, and in books published by Cambridge University Press, Houghton Mifflin, and Random House.

Randy is a big fan of E. Basil St. Blaise's caustic revues and has been mildly delighted to illustrate them for the last five years.

Martin Kozlowski

Since 1980 Martin Kozlowski has chronicled the social and political scenes in a wide range of publications including *Barron's*, the *National Law Journal*, the *New York Times*, *Newsday* and the *Wall Street Journal*.

He art directs and contributes to the weekly editorial illustration service *inxart. com*. His comic strips have appeared in a variety of publications including *Fortune* and the *Daily Star* in Beirut, Lebanon. His work has appeared in numerous exhibitions including shows in New York, Paris, Santa Fe, Calgary and Warsaw. He is the editor-in-chief of nowwhatmedia.com. His artwork herein is signed KOZ.

2008

Javier Bardem prods Oscar to reconsider *No Country For Old Men*

Academy Awards Best Picture

No Country For Old Men — Paean Coens.

....

Meet the Spartans — Greeks' havoc.

Cloverfield — Godzilla vs. Digicamera.

Cassandra's Dream — Woody's annual chuck up.

Hannah Montana & Miley Cyrus: Best of Both Worlds Concert — Tweenie roast.

The Eye — Sore.

....

Over Her Dead Body — Where I'm doing a jig.

Vince Vaughn's Wild West Comedy Show — Prattle drive.

Welcome Home, Roscoe Jenkins — Kith my ass.

Fool's Gold — Romcomatose.

In Bruges — Brussels prats.

The Hottie & the Nottie — The bimbo & the dimbo.

Definitely, Maybe — Not, assuredly.

Jack Black suffers ejection by Mos Def in *Be Kind Rewind*

....

Be Kind Rewind — This case erase.

Jumper — Jump! Jump!

The Spiderwick Chronicles — Fairy to middling.

Vantage Point — Worm's-eye view.

Charlie Bartlett — Dose off.

Witless Protection — Save cracker.

The Counterfeiters — Forge focus.

Step Up 2 the Streets — From the gutter.

....

George A. Romero's Diary of the Dead — PDOA.

Semi-Pro — Nothing but *nyet*.

Penelope — Twist and snout.

The Other Boleyn Girl — With the skinnier neck.

City of Men — Rio deGenerates.

Beyond Belief — Tenets, anyone?

10,000 B.C. — Before Coherence.

The Bank Job — Withdrawal symptoms.

Horton Hears a Who — Ask "Why?"

Married Life — Atrothcious.

Miss Pettigrew Lives for a Day — Spinster cycle.

Drillbit Taylor — Boring.

Tyler Perry's Meet the Browns — Acute case of Perrytonitis.

Sputnik Mania — Orbit curiosity.

Doomsday — Road Wearier.

Heartbeat Detector — Bum ticker.

Funny Games — You lose!

Flawless — Karat and shtick.

American Zombie — Dead, white and blue.

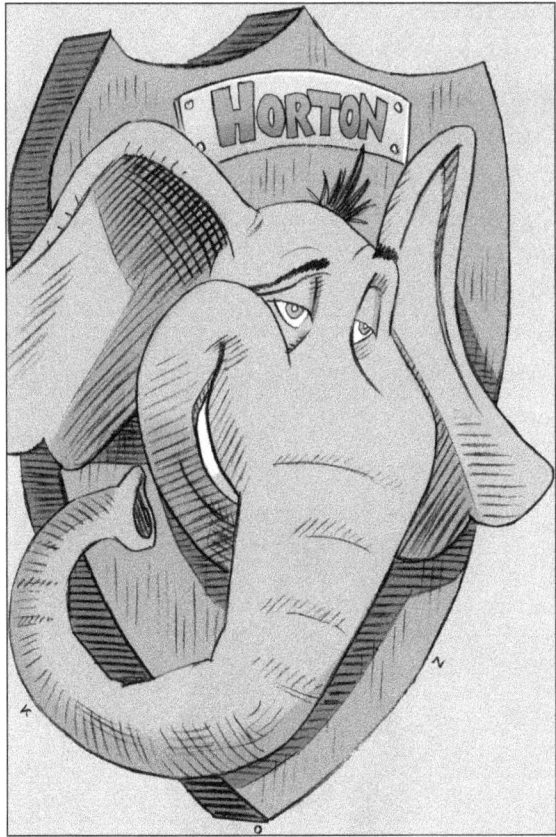

Horton mounted in *Horton Hears a Who*

....

Run, Fat Boy, Run — Pegg in a poke.

Stop-Loss — Droop rotation.

21 — Hit me…when it's over.

Superhero Movie — Sequel to none.

Leatherheads — Take a hike.

Shine a Light — Where the sun don't shine.

Sex and Death 101 — Flunk U.

Nim's Island — Takes atoll.

Ruins — My evening.

Smart People — Not in the audience.

Street Kings — Block heads.

Prom Night — Rended tux.

The Take — *Eww*-Haul.

Forbidden Kingdom — Chop schlocky.

Forgetting Sarah Marshall — Done.

88 Minutes — Gee, that is pretty fast to write a script.

Harold and Kumar Escape from Guantanamo Bay — But I thought they ran the place.

Redbelt — Redbull.

Deception — Scambags.

Made of Honor — Or a synthetic substitute thereof.

Baby Mama — Pee didie.

Tina Fey and her surrogate, Amy Poehler, in *Baby Mama*

Robert Downey Jr. emotes in *Iron Man*

Iron Man — Less than riveting.

Chronicles of Narnia: Prince Caspian — You fight like a girl…nar, nar, nar, nar, nar…nia.

The Favor — Does me no.

Graduation — College-boned.

Speed Racer — Or: Zippy the Pinhead.

What Happens in Vegas — Strip maul.

The Babysitters — Tit for tot.

Foot Fist Way — Tae Kwan Dope.

....

Sex and the City — Ovary familiar.

How the Garcia Girls Spent Their Summers — Chica flick.

Sangre de Mi Sangre — Bloody awful.

Indiana Jones and the Kingdom of the Crystal Skull — Serial killer.

The Strangers — As tense as a numb sphincter.

Bigger, Stronger, Faster* — The 'Roid Stuff.

Miss Conception — Her biological crock.

War Inc. — Stale matériel.

You Don't Mess with the Zohan — Schmo dry.

Mongol — Horde times.

Sara Jessica Parker & Mr. Big in *Sex and the City*

The Honeymooner Hulk

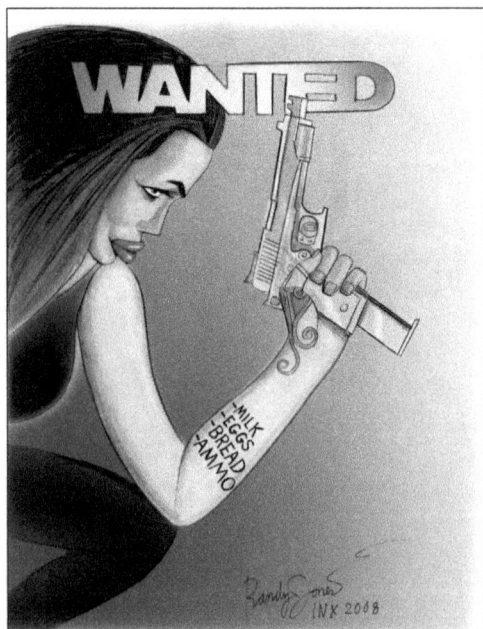

Angelina Jolie checks her hit list in *Wanted*

The Incredible Hulk — Green stomps.

Kung Fu Panda — The bear minimum.

The Happening — Shyamalan-a-ding-dong.

Baghead — Anonymous botch.

The Last Mistress — Pantaloony.

The Love Guru — Swami dearest.

Get Smart — Badder CONTROL.

Kitt Kittredge: An American Girl — Pure dumb pluck.

Finding Amanda — Slut machine.

....

Wanted — Dud or alive.

WALL*E — FOLL*E.

Encounters at the End of the World — Frigid dare.

Hancock — Smith & wussin'.

Tell No One — My lids are sealed.

Gonzo: The Life and Work of Dr. Hunter S. Thompson — Fear and lauding.

Journey to the Center of the Earth — Cores light.

Meet Dave — Itty Murphy.

Another Gay Sequel — Like *Mission: Impossible III*?

Swing Vote — Pollish joke.

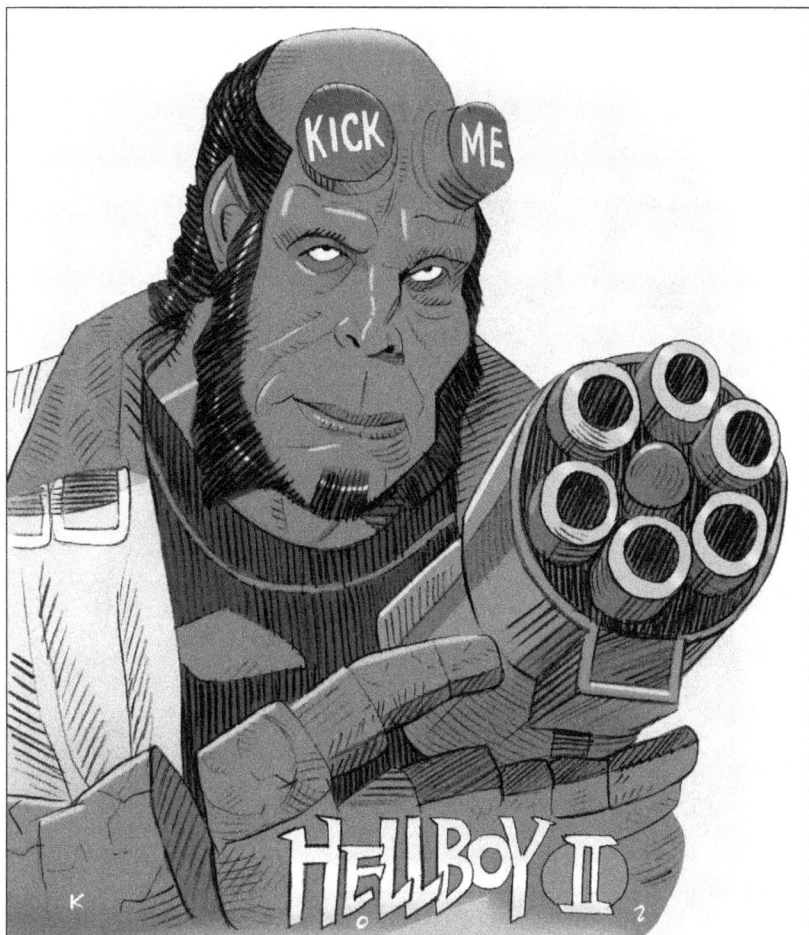

Ron Perlman as the original horndog in *Hellboy 2*

Hellboy II: The Golden Army — Red socks.

Mamma Mia! — ABBA cadaver.

Space Chimps — Banana dickery.

Before I Forget — Too late.

Step Brothers — Made from scraps.

The X-Files: I Want to Believe — That makes one of us.

American Teen — Teeny weenies.

Brideshead Revisited — Waugh is Hell.

Bustin' Down the Door — To exit the theatre.

No Regret — If you don't count the ticket price.

Heath Ledger jokes around with Christian Bale in *The Dark Knight*

....

The Dark Knight — From bat to worse.

Man on Wire — Tiptoe through the two towers.

The Mummy: Tomb of the Dragon Emperor — Inter the Dragon.

Pineapple Express — Pot holes.

Sisterhood of the Traveling Pants 2 — The britches' back.

Elegy — Lamentable.

Bottle Shock — Arse and carafes.

Hell Ride — Spayed demon.

Vicky Cristina Barcelona — Spanish bomblet.

The Clone Wars — Dub and Dubber.

The Rocker — Lame chops.

The House Bunny — A Hef wit.

Death Race — They've got to be skidding.

The Longshots — Limp Kidzpik.

Cthulhu — Lovecraft warnings.

Hamlet 2 — No holds Bard.

Babylon A.D. — D.

Traitor — Do the rat thing.

College — Drop out.

Disaster Movie — Calamity jape.

Sukiyaki Western Django — Samurai'dem, cowboy.

Bangkok Dangerous — Thai die.

Blindness — Eye give up.

Jack Brooks: Monster Slayer — Army of Dorkness.

The Pool — Swim pickings.

Tropic Thunder — CGI Joe.

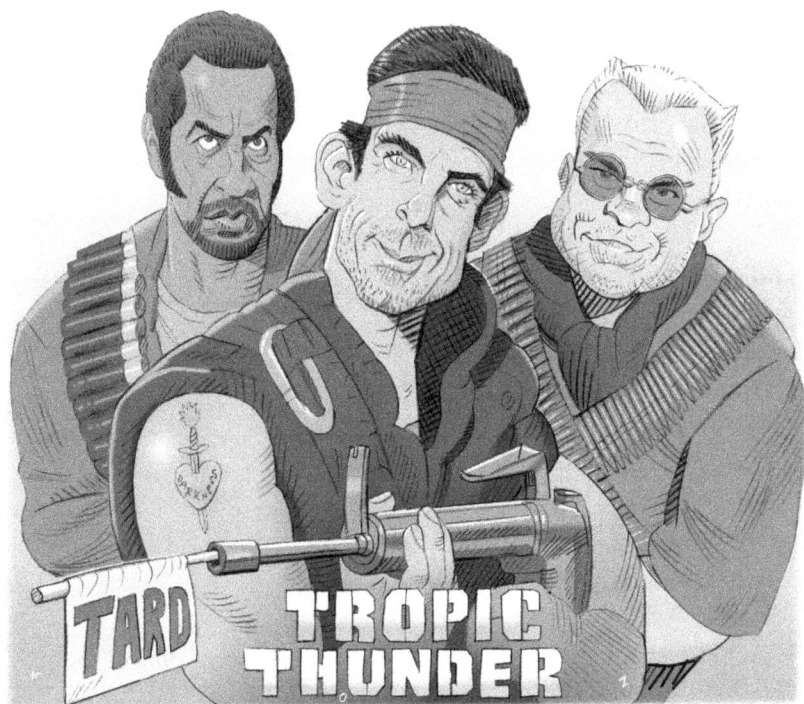

Robert Downey Jr., Ben Stiller & Jack Black go ballistic in *Tropic Thunder*

Uncured hams De Niro & Pacino in *Righteous Kill*

Righteous Kill — So both careers deserve to die?

Burn After Reading — For Your *Oys* Only.

The Women — Estrogen fizz.

Tyler Perry's The Family That Preys — Faint *Preys*.

Eagle Eye — Aerie-fairy.

Nights in Rodanthe — An old man's fanthe.

House of the Sleeping Beauties — Sleep depraved.

Miracle at St. Anna — Effed troop.

Choke — Extremely hard to swallow.

Lakeview Terrace — Won't you beat my neighbor?

Igor — Ho hump.

Appaloosa — *Aww*, poor loser.

....

Ghost Town — Whine and spirits.

The Duchess — Noble gas.

Battle in Seattle — Left, left, left, riot, left.

Beverly Hills Chihuahua — Perrotechnics.

Rachel Getting Married — Aisle be damned.

Flash of Genius — Swiper blades.

How to Lose Friends & Alienate People — Invite them to see this.

Nick & Norah's Infinite Playlist — Shuffle bored.

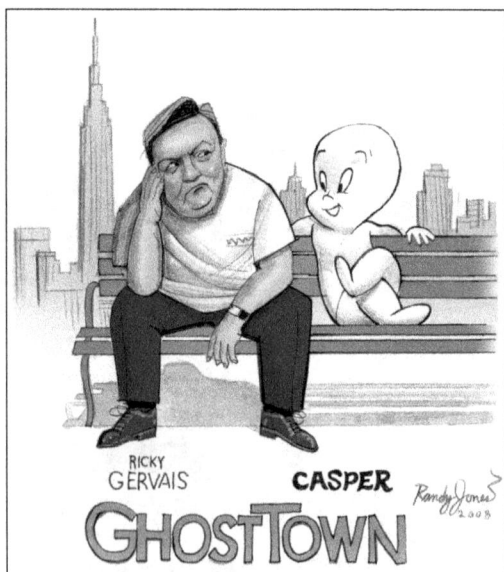

RICKY GERVAIS   CASPER

GHOSTTOWN

Ricky Gervais and spectral costar in *Ghost Town*

Bill Maher interviews the Almighty in *Religulous*

Religulous — Blasphemoronic.

Allah Made Me Funny — Hajji-har-har.

Body of Lies — Err Jordan.

City of Ember — Ashinine.

Quarantine — City sicker.

Happy-Go-Lucky — Cheery picker.

Max Payne — Min Pleasure.

Secret Life of Bees — All warm and buzzy.

What Just Happened — Pic's disease.

Not Your Typical Bigfoot Movie — Homina homina hominid!

Filth and Wisdom — Lazy Madonna.

High School Musical 3: Senior Year — Degrade point average.

Pride and Glory — Badge to the bone.

Saw V — Dismembers only.

Let the Right One In — The left one's already seen it.

The real deal in the period piece *W.*

....

W. — C.

Changeling — Tyke-away.

RocknRolla — Ritchie wretch.

The Haunting of Molly Hartley — Crapparitions.

Soul Men — Dead singers.

Role Models — Mentor cases.

Madagascar: Escape 2 Africa — Jungle rot.

The Boy in the Striped Pajamas — Jackboot camp.

Quantum of Solace — *Quantum* leaks.

Slumdog Millionaire — Makin' rupee.

A Christmas Tale — Nöel cowards.

The Alphabet Killer — Gory spelling.

Australia — *Ewws* and Oz.

The Beautiful Truth — The topic of cancer.

Seth Rogen & Elizabeth Banks zoom out in *Zack and Miri Make a Porno*

....

Zack and Miri Make a Porno — Dude raunch.

What Doesn't Kill You — Makes you dumber.

Bolt — From the theatre.

Milk — Toast.

Four Christmases — Like I gift a shit.

Transporter 3 — Tote drag.

Cadillac Records — The triumph of Deville.

Punisher: War Zone — My maim man.

Frost/Nixon — Shitchat.

Twilight — Dusk devils.

The Day the Earth Stood Still — And nodded off.

Nothing Like the Holidays — Feliz naive dud.

Doubt — Church's chicken.

Wendy and Lucy — Dog and phony show.

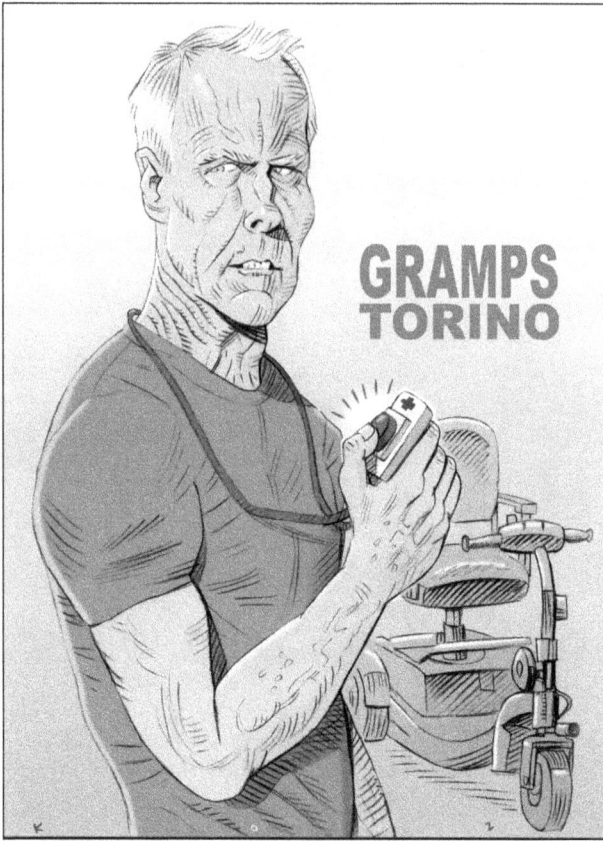

GRAMPS TORINO

Clint Eastwood and his wheels in *Grand Torino*

Gran Torino — Driver's id.

Yes Man — No sir.

The Reader — From left to Reich.

Marley & Me — Pup crawl.

Che — It ain't so.

Bedtime Stories — If you like nightmares.

Seven Pounds — That's a lot of baloney.

The Tale of Despereaux — Three bland mice.

The Wrestler — Pins and needless.

Harvard Beats Yale 29-29 — Jivy League.

Nothing But the Truth — Plame and fancy.

The Spirit — My city screams…with laughter.

Scott Walker: 30 Century Man — Icky pop.

Timecrimes — Like stealing 88 mins. of my life.

The Curious Case of Benjamin Button — Ass backwards.

Valkyrie — SSination plot.

Revolutionary Road — Petit-bushwa.

Last Chance Harvey — Dustbin Hoffman.

Waltz With Bashir — Beirut of all evil.

Where God Put His Shoes — After he stepped in this.

2009

Sean Penn of *Milk* pins Mickey Rourke of *The Wrestler* for Best Actor

Academy Awards Best Picture

Slumdog Millionaire — Shrimp Oscar.

....

Bride Wars — Something borrowed, something blew.

The Unborn — Belly whopper.

The Pervert's Guide to Cinema — Not a dry seat in the house.

Hotel For Dogs — Red Ruff Inn.

My Bloody Valentine 3D — Heart-chopping.

Notorious — B.I.G. deal.

Inkheart — Prints of darkness.

Underworld: Rise of the Lycans — Werewolf blitzer.

Crips and Bloods: Made in America — The gangs, all here.

Dealing and Wheeling in Small Arms — On the piece plan.

Taken — With a grain of assault.

Vigilant Kevin James in *Paul Blart: Mall Cop*

Frosty Renee Zellweger in *New in Town*

Paul Blart: Mall Cop — Exactly as funny as his name.

Uninvited — Guest of horror.

Pink Panther 2 — Clouseau, but no cigar.

Coraline — The sorrow and the kiddie.

He's Just Not That Into You — Makes two of us.

Push — Over.

Polanski — Roman scandals.

The International — House of fruitcakes.

Friday the 13th — Jason beastly.

Confessions of a Shopaholic — Consumer fraught.

The Caller — Disconnect.

Gomorrah — Sod 'em.

....

New in Town — Blows in.

Fired Up! — A rah deal.

Garrison Keillor: The Man on the Radio in the Red Shoes — A dreary home companion.

Jonas Brothers: The 3D Concert Experience — Hey, hey we're the Honkees.

Two Lovers — Bicupids.

Bob Funk — *Funk* dat.

Everlasting Moments — Eon, eon, ohh!

Explicit Ills — Plain sick.

Fados — Not fado way.

Horsemen — Apocalypse no.

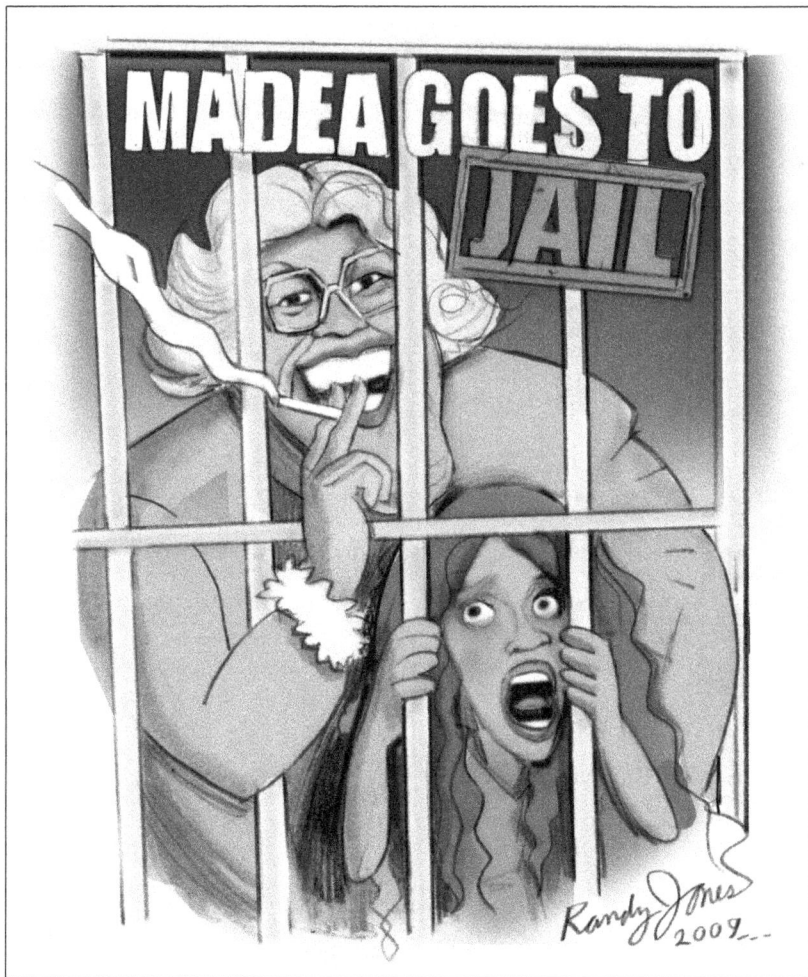

Cross-dresser Tyler ends up in the can in *Madea Goes to Jail*

....

Tyler Perry's Madea Goes to Jail — A clinker.

Race to Witch Mountain — Rock slide.

Miss March — Miss every month.

The Last House on the Left — Where Rachel Maddow lives.

Alexander the Last — At least, no sequels.

The Cake Eaters — Let's just say the frosting ain't chocolate.

Valentino: the Last Emperor — With no clothes.

The Perfect Sleep — I did wake up once to use the rest room.

Silk Spectre II, Dr. Manhattan & Rorschach look sharp in *Watchmen*

....

Watchmen — Comic con.

I Love You, Man — Mal bonding.

Duplicity — Asspionage.

Knowing — No win.

The Great Buck Howard — Beefing John Malkovich.

The Haunting in Connecticut — Rickety-boo.

12 Rounds — A technical nod out.

American Swing — Home of the swapper.

The Education of Charley Banks — Learner and low.

Bart Got a Room — Prom dunce.

Alien Trespass — Shit Came From Outer Space.

Enlighten Up! — Yogi bore.

Adventureland — Skeeve ball.

Fast & Furious — Wheelie, wheelie bad.

The Mysteries of Pittsburgh — Pitt bull.

Monsters vs. Aliens — Monsters, Ick.

Ginormica demonstrates her gynormity to Gallaxar in *Monsters vs. Aliens*

The Pope's Toilet — Il Poopa.

Hannah Montana: The Movie — Miley's People.

Observe and Report — OK. It's a car wreck.

Dragonball: Evolution — Lizardnuts.

Anvil! The Story of Anvil — They're hammered.

In a Dream — Nap sack.

State of Play — *Play* dead.

Crank: High Voltage — Guilty as charged.

17 Again — Rerunt.

Oblivion — Nowhere, man.

The Soloist — So low.

Earth — Orb bits.

Obsessed — Nad philanders.

X-Men Origins: Wolverine — Claws and effect.

....

Liev Schreiber's Sabretooth shaves Hugh Jackman in *X-Men Origins: Wolverine*

Zachary Quinto & Chris Pine in the Shatnerless *Star Trek*

···

Star Trek — W.U.S.S. enterprise.

Next Day Air — It's stale.

Adoration — Odor ration.

Audience of One — If they're lucky.

Fighting — Back a yawn.

The Garden — Patch work.

The Informer — Leaker license.

Outrage — Homo electus.

Battle for Terra — *Terra* bull.

Ghosts of Girlfriends Past — Dates of yore.

Angels & Demons — The papal chase.

Management — Motel Sex.

Brothers Bloom — And wither.

Terminator Salvation — Savior money.

Carl Fredricksen and the blimp-like Carl in *Up*

Up — Yours.

Drag Me to Hell — *D'oh* Raimi.

The Art of Being Straight — The thin gay line.

Departures — Leave and let die.

Night at the Museum: Battle of the Smithsonian — Admission impossible.

Dance Flick — Hit me with your rhythm shtick.

The Girlfriend Experience — Heave ho.

....

Land of the Lost — Primordial *oohs*.

The Hangover — The bachelor retch.

My Life in Ruins — Tour down.

Year One — Audience zero.

The Proposal — Engagement wrung.

Whatever Works — Leery David.

My Sister's Keeper — Not a keeper.

Surveillance — Nothing much to see.

....

Cheri — Vanilla.

Public Enemies — America's Least Wanted.

Ice Age: Dawn of the Dinosaurs — The Cretinaceous Period.

I Hate Valentine's Day — Heart-ons.

Beaches of Agnes — Mal de merde.

I Love You, Beth Cooper — Hatin' Panetierre.

Humpday — Buggers off.

The Hurt Locker — Bomb squat.

Tunnel inspector John Travolta in *The Taking of Pelham 123*

....

The Taking of Pelham 123 — Local yokels.

Transformers: Revenge of the Fallen — Botlickers.

....

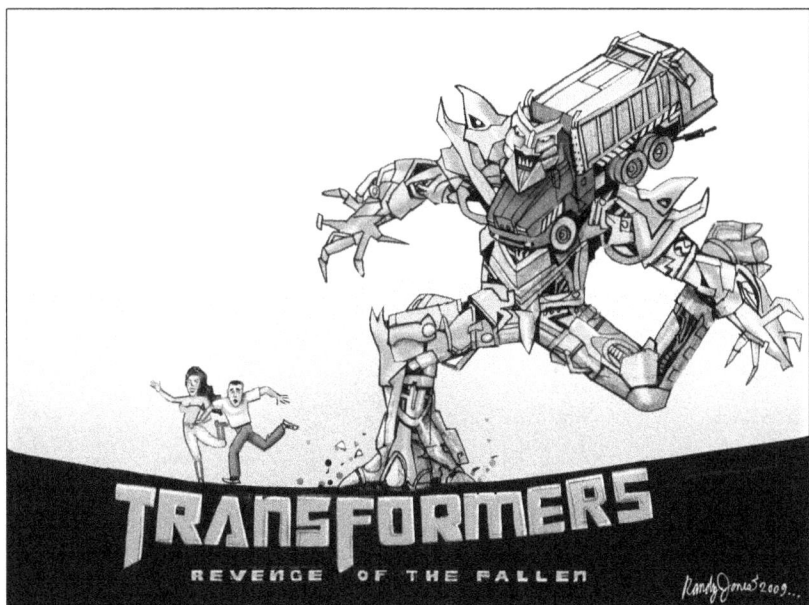

A Decepticon tails Megan Fox & Shia LaBeouf in *Transformers: Revenge of the Fallen*

Brüno with more than just a touch of Borat

Brüno — Homo erratic.

Blood: The Last Vampire — O, negative!

Weather Girl — Hail Mary.

The Cove — Bayside the point.

(500) Days of Summer — Sweat large.

G-Force — Giddy pigs.

Orphan — The urchin of menace.

The Ugly Truth — *Truth* decay.

The Answer Man — Highly questionable.

In the Loop — Circle jerks.

Funny People — Hardly har har.

The Collector — Of lint.

Aliens in the Attic — Loft in space.

Adam — Shame.

Ghosted — No one would take credit.

Fragments — Blows chunks.

I Sell the Dead — Insurance.

G.I. Joe: The Rise of Cobra — Toy soldiers.

A Perfect Getaway — Escape hybrid.

....

Cold Souls — Spirit kvetcher.

My Führer — Sick heil.

The Goods — The bads and the uglies.

District 9 — Interned for the worst.

The Time Traveler's Wife — Hour lady of perpetual torment.

Bandslam — Glandslam.

The September Issue — *Vogue* elephant.

Harry Potter and the Half-Blood Prince — And the half-ass script.

....

Daniel Radcliffe's Harry tries to outwit Ralph Fiennes' Voldemort with the old "I stole your nose" trick in *Harry Potter and the Half-Blood Prince*

Julie & Julia — Child abuse.

Taking Woodstock — And making it dull.

Halloween II — Boogey loogey.

The Horse Boy — Colt case.

Big Fan — Rah, rah, sick goombah.

Extract — Remove with tweezers.

All About Steve — Sandra bollix.

Gamer — Gamey.

Amy Adams tries Meryl Streep's fixins in *Julie & Julia*

Tyler Perry's I Can Do Bad All By Myself — And here's proof.

Orgies and the Meaning of Life — Aww, geez.

Beyond a Reasonable Doubt — I'm convinced it blows.

#9 in the side pocket in *9*

9 — 11.

Sorority Row — Cherry Pi.

Whiteout — Must've covered the screenplay.

The Other Man — Cuckold doodle doo.

Give Me Your Hand — And I'll pull your finger.

The Most Dangerous Man in America: Daniel Ellsberg and the Pentagon Papers — The Namburglar.

Precious — Little.

Tarantino and Pitt prepare to scalp the audience in *Inglourious Basterds*

....

Inglourious Basterds — Nutzi hunters.

Informant! — The inside dope.

Jennifer's Body — Gross anatomy.

Love Happens — Venereal dizzies.

The Burning Plain — Crash.

Bright Star — Ode, the pain!

35 Shots of Rum — Should get you through this.

....

Surrogates — Proxymorons.

Pandorum — Fanboy slim.

Fame — Nerdy dancing.

The Boys Are Back — Male pattern ball-less.

Capitalism: A Love Story — Marxist research.

The Invention of Lying — Fibulous.

Whip It — Roller twerpy.

A Serious Man — A mazel tov cocktail.

The title character delivers big time in *Astroboy*

Astro Boy — Hate manga.

Couples Retreat — Borer borer.

The Damned United — Brit kickers.

Bronson — Balonious assault.

Rocket Singh: Salesman of the Year — Sikh and destroy.

Ball Don't Lie — Technically foul.

Adventures of Power — Business weak.

Disengagement — The butt end of the affair.

Where the Wild Things Are — Maurice, send *Ack!*

An Education — Crème de la cram.

....

Trucker — A looong haul.

St. Trinian's — Miss behavior.

Free Style — Track and ruin.

Stark Raving Black — Chary Lewis.

Cloudy With a Chance of Meatballs — Meatierology.

Toy Story 3D — Cold play.

Law Abiding Citizen — Brute farce.

The Stepfather — Pop's off.

The Maid — Domestic disturbance.

Black Dynamite — Crank *Shaft*.

Woody Harrelson prepares to blast a ravening ghoul in *Zombieland*

Zombieland — Undead-developed.

Food Beware: The French Organic Revolution — *Fruits* at last!

Cirque du Freak: The Vampire's Assistant — Fangboy.

Michael Jackson's This Is It — Beat *It*…with a stick.

Amelia — Err hard.

Saw VI — Cut and died.

Antichrist — *Anti* tanks.

Boondock Saints II: All Saints Day — Sin shitty.

The House of the Devil — Split-evil.

Gentlemen Broncos — Dork and pony show.

The Men Who Stare at Goats — Nanny 911.

The Box — Square.

Jacko's Danse Macabre in *This Is It*

Bullock tackles Aaron in *The Blind Side*

The Blind Side — The Joy of Sacks.

Disney's A Christmas Carol — Scrooge the pooch.

The Fourth Kind — Silly *Fourth.*

2012 — Mayan shaft.

Fantastic Mr. Fox — A Dahl headache.

Pirate Radio — Ham fisted.

Dare — There's no dare there.

The Road — Not takin'.

The Messenger — Casualty assurance.

The Twilight Saga: New Moon — Rapidly wanes.

Planet 51 — Out of 50.

....

Bad Lieutenant: Port of Call New Orleans — Rabid Cage.

Old Dogs — Barker loungers.

Ninja Assassin — Happily sever after.

Me and Orson Welles — *Welles*: forgo.

The Princess and the Frog — Unhip hop.

Everybody's Fine — Once they exit the theatre.

Up In the Air — Flight dreck.

Brothers — Sib code.

Paranormal Activity — The phantom minus.

Armored — Robber barren.

The Last Station — Tolstoy Story.

Invictus — Nelson man duller.

The Lovely Bones — Spineless.

A Single Man — Who's on Firth?

Tenderness — In the groin area.

Breaking Point — I reached it at the fifteen minute mark.

Nine — Nein.

Did You Hear About the Morgans? — No, and you won't.

Crazy Heart — Strum und drang.

Ricky — Crib-tickler.

Sherlock Holmes — Holmes wrecker.

It's Complicated — If you're simple.

....

Alvin and the Chipmunks: The Squeakquel — More a suckquel.

The Imaginarium of Dr. Parnassus — Bomb of Gilliam.

The White Ribbon — Village of the dimmed.

Young Victoria — We are not amused.

Brief Interviews With Hideous Men — Where's the Limbaugh clip?

Coco Before Chanel — And before 'nuts'.

My Son, My Son, What Have Ye Done? — Werner herds hog.

Avatar — Army vs. Na'vi.

....

The mystical, magical blue folk in *Avatar*

2010

Christoph Waltz of *Inglourious Basterds*, Sandra Bullock of The *Blind Side*, and Carl Fredricksen of *Up* in friendly competition with Jake Sully of *Avatar*

Academy Awards Best Picture

The Hurt Locker — Oscar de la rental.

....

Daybreakers — Dawn of the dud.

Leap Year — Off a bridge.

Youth in Revolt — Rebel yelp.

The Spy Next Door — Jerky Chan.

44 Inch Chest — Tremendous boobs.

Fish Tank — Surface scum.

Waiting for Armageddon — Rapture head around this.

Extraordinary Measures — May be required to revive you.

The Tooth Fairy — Yank it.

Legion — *Urgh*angels.

A Room and a Half — W/No Vu.

Creation — Unnatural selection.

The Girl on the Train — A commute point.

Edge of Darkness — It's just your eyelids closing.

When in Rome — Do as the romcoms do.

Saint John of Las Vegas — *John* the Craptist.

North Face — Mountain. Pass.

Still Bill — Right, shut him up.

From Paris With Love — And scabies.

Dear John — The wimping post.

District 13: Ultimatum — Parkour posey.

Ajami — Acidic Jews.

Terribly Happy — Happily terrible.

Red Riding — Hoods.

Percy Jackson & the Olympians: The Lightning Thief — Up a Greek.

Valentine's Day — Germs of endearment.

The Book of Eli — Eli-Eli-*Ohhh*.

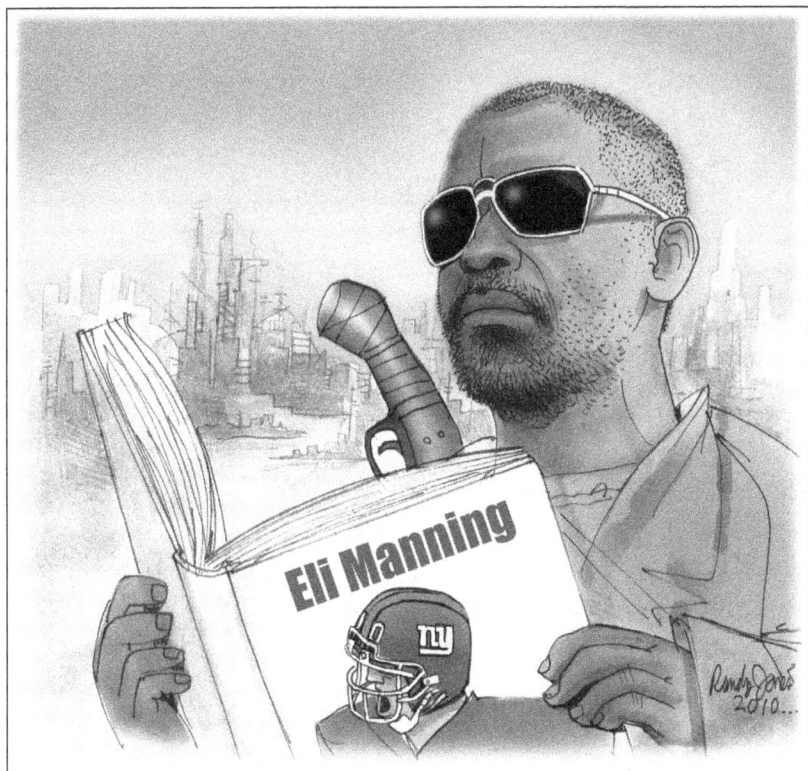

Denzell Washington bones up on his sacred text in *The Book of Eli*

Benicio Del Toro as Lawrence Talbot, son of Anthony Hopkins' Sir John Talbot, seeks relief from his curse in *The Wolfman*

....

The Wolfman — An ass howl.

The Ghost Writer — Bio degradable.

Celine: Through the Eyes of the World — And through its colon.

A Prophet — And loss.

Cop Out — Dick jokes.

The Crazies — The teabaggers have their own movie?

The Art of the Steal — Barnes burner.

Defendor — Offendor.

The Yellow Handkerchief — Full of snots.

The Good Guy — Finishes last.

Shutter Island — Shutter theatre.

Brooklyn's Finest — Poor Brooklyn.

Green Zone — Natural Bourne killers.

Remember Me — Starring What's-his-face.

Our Family Wedding — Panic groom.

She's Out of My League — Pee-wee vermin.

Leonardo DiCaprio discovers the awful secret behind Door 67 in *Shutter Island*

The Cry of the Owl — *Hoo*-boy!

The Exploding Girl — Boom box.

....

Alice in Wonderland — Alice in chintz.

City Island — Bronx jeer.

The Bounty Hunter — Dog: *The Bounty Hunter.*

Repo Men — Whatever repossessed them?

Diary of a Wimpy Kid — Spaz cadet.

The Red Baron — Meet the fokkers.

Greenberg — Schlemiel plan.

The Runaways — Jett blew.

Johnny Depp's Mad Hatter welcomes an uninvited guest in *Alice in Wonderland*

The Girl with the Dragon Tattoo — Tat for tit.

Vincere — Il Ducebag.

Hot Tub Time Machine — Ladies and germs.

How to Train Your Dragon — How to drain your lizard.

Bluebeard — Choke mate.

Chloe — Schmoe.

Ca$h — For clunkers.

Clash of the Titans — Perseus wears spots, the Kraken, stripes.

....

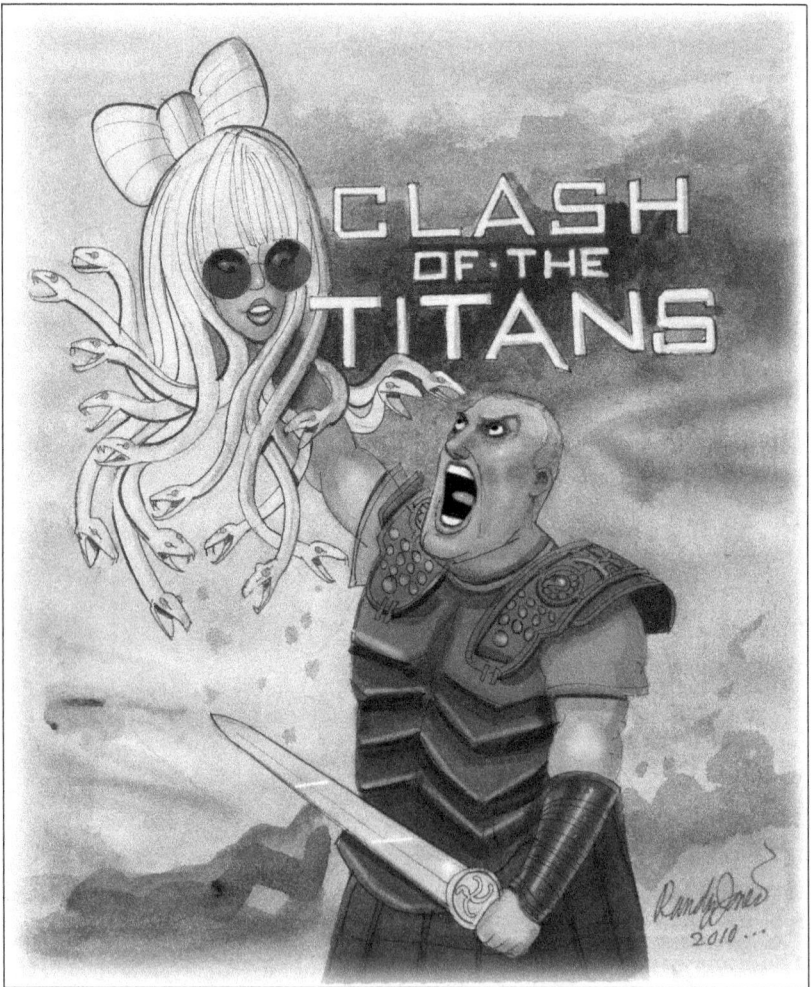

Sam Worthington as Perseus slays the Gaga Gorgon in *Clash of the Titans*

The Eclipse — The ghost whimperer.

The Last Song — Refrain yourself.

Tyler Perry's Why Did I Get Married Too — Too who?

Date Night — Date on arrival.

After.Life — Decease and desist.

Don McKay — *McKay* mouse.

The Greatest — Compared to what?

Kick-Ass — Kiss-ass.

....

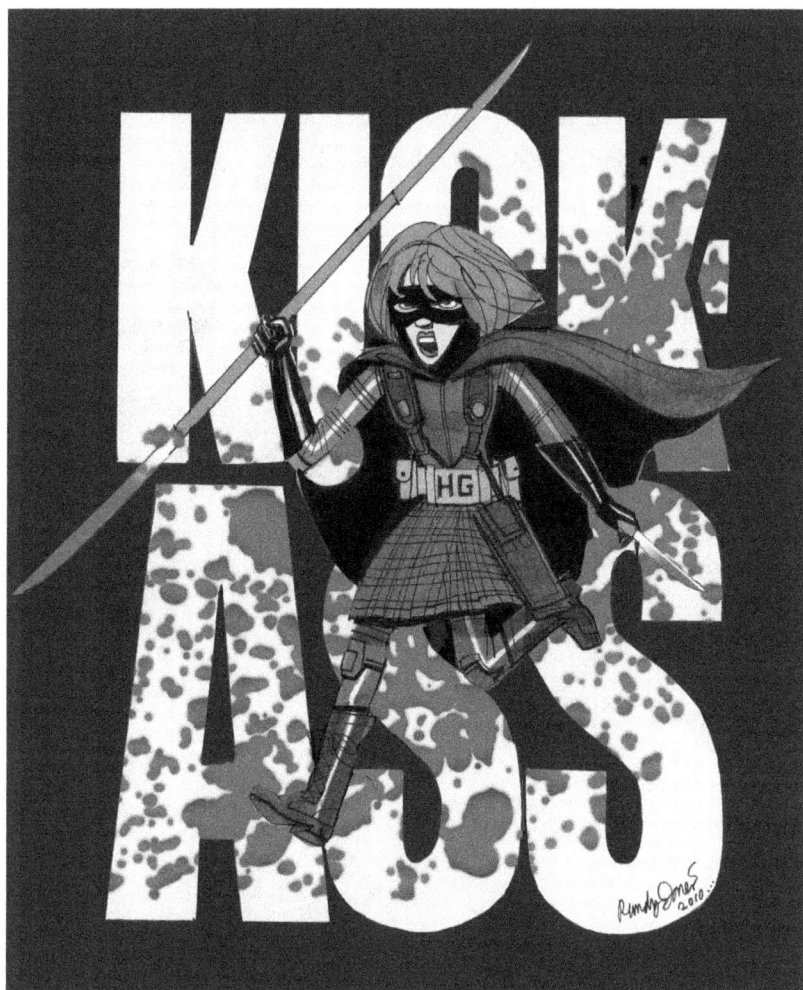

Chloë Grace Moretz as Hit-Girl spills blood in *Kick-Ass*

Death at a Funeral — Bury, bury bad.

The Joneses — Don't keep up with them.

The City of Your Final Destination — Ivory sop.

In My Sleep — I directed this.

Exit Through the Gift Shop — Banksy driver.

Behind the Burly Q — Bum and grind.

The Losers — Or *The Audience*.

Oceans — Sea whirled.

Accidents Happen — On your rug.

Best Worst Movie — *Best*, bye.

Boogie Woogie — *Boogie* nits.

Kenny Chesney: Summer in 3D — Kenny? Geez.

My Boyfriend's Girlfriend — Ardor nonsense.

The Good, the Bad, the Weird — Kinks of Leone.

....

The Back-up Plan — Plan Z.

Furry Vengence — Borscht Pelt.

A Nightmare on Elm Street — Freddy offender.

Casino Jack and the United States of Money — Abramoff the record.

Harry Brown — With a whacking Caine.

Anton Chekhov's The Duel — Pistol wimped.

The Good Heart — Beat.

Jennifer Lopez's back in *The Back-up Plan*

Russell Crowe as a pugnacious *Robin Hood*

....

Robin Hood — Bow diddly.

Please Give — Me a break.

Phish 3D — Doobie, doobie, doobie.

TiMER — Set to endless.

Multiple Sarcasms — Scoff flaws.

The Human Centipede — Crappy-crawly.

Babies — Doo-doo, dada.

....

Ironman 2 — Rusty nil.

OSS 117: Lost in Rio — A dumbbell agent.

Happiness Runs — Down your leg.

The Oath — Swear off it.

Letters to Juliet — Where fart thou, Romeo?

Just Wright — Utterly rong.

Princess Kaiulani — Hawaii? Not so good.

Shrek & Friends are finally terminated in *Shrek Forever After*

....

Shrek Forever After — Shrek and ruin.

MacGruber — Lower Forte.

180 Degrees South — Directile dysfunction.

After the Cup — For the athletic supporter.

Solitary Man — Lone shark.

Looking for Eric — Eric crapped on.

Sex & the City 2 — Carrie on and on.

Agora — A bare market.

Micmacs — Muckmix.

Survival of the Dead — They overcame burybury.

Jake Gyllenhaal as Dastan faces the evil ruler in *Prince of Persia: Sands of Time*

Prince of Persia: The Sands of Time — Dune buggy.

Joan Rivers: A Piece of Work — Yenta laughing.

Picasso and Braque Go to the Movies — The Cubist little things.

Get Him to the Greek — Brand *Ecchs*.

Splice — Of life.

Killers — Slayed low.

Marmaduke — Cur-*plop*.

Ondine — Nymph skulls.

Coco Chanel & Igor Stravinsky — The Riot of Spring.

The comedy legend puts on her game face in *Joan Rivers: A Piece of Work*

The A-Team — Unsolved Mister T.

The Karate Kid — *Blech* belt.

The Lottery — A whole lotto nothing.

8: The Mormon Proposition — Annul a gay.

Jonah Hex — *Hex* marks the splotch.

Cyrus — Mealy *Cyrus*.

The Killer Inside Me — Curled up in the fatal position.

Lovers of Hate — Will love this.

Let It Rain — Soppy.

Stonewall Uprising — Preaching to the queer.

Toy Story 3 — Play-doo.

....

Woody, Jessie, Buzz Lightyear, Hamm, Mr. & Mrs. Potato Head, Rex, Slinky Dog, Bullseye and the Little Green Men are played out in *Toy Story 3*

Robert Pattinson & Taylor Lautner prove they have acting chops as they pretend to salivate over Kristen Stewart in *The Twilight Saga: Eclipse*

The Twilight Saga: Eclipse — Moon drivel.

Knight and Day — You are the wan.

Grown Ups — Thrown ups.

Restrepo — Gaffehanistan.

Dogtooth — Gnashville.

Out in the Silence — A twink and a nod.

South of the Border — Bolívar of broken dreams.

Wild Grass — Now you know what the director was smoking.

The Last Airbender — He can really flex his sphincter.

Love Ranch — Dud *Ranch*.

Only When I Dance — Pas de douche.

Predators — Let us prey.

The Kids Are All Right — Mommy queerest.

The Girl Who Played With Fire — Burning bush.

Winnebago Man — RV wallbanger.

Grease Sing-a-Long — You're the one that I won't.

[REC]2 — A nervous [REC].

The Sorcerer's Apprentice — Cheese wiz.

Inception — Dream weeper.

Standing Ovation — A hand job.

Valhalla Rising — You might feel Norse-ish.

....

Salt — And battery.

Ramona and Beezus — Skid sister.

Life During Wartime — It ain't no party.

Jean-Michel Basquiat — A Basquiat case.

What's the Matter With Kansas? — Could be a miniseries.

Hugh Hefner: Playboy, Activist and Rebel — Hef cocked.

Despicable Me — Disposable you.

....

Gru "flogs his minion" in *Despicable Me*

The Last Exorcism or *Lindsay Lohan on Saturday Night*

The Last Exorcism — Devil washup.

Dinner for Schmucks — Jerky.

Charlie St. Cloud — His brother's cryptkeeper.

Get Low — This already has.

Cats & Dogs: The Revenge of Kitty Galore — Insanity claws.

The Extra Man — Superfluous.

The Other Guys — N.Y.P.U.

Step Up 3-D — Twerpsichorean.

Middle Men — Porn brokers.

The Disappearance of Alice Creed — Appall-o *Creed*.

Flipped — Flopped.

The Oxford Murders — The shoes are killing them.

The Expendables — Ol' gore.

Scott Pilgrim vs. the World — Dork fight.

Eat, Pray, Love — Sneer.

Animal Kingdom — Cops and rotters.

Tales from Earthsea — Looney toons.

The People I've Slept With — In the theatre showing this.

....

They Came to Play — Pianist envy.

Takers — Leavers.

Centurion — Romecom.

Mesrine: L'ennemi Public No 1 — French dip.

The Switch — Sperm wail.

Piranha 3-D — Piscine contest.

Nanny McPhee Returns — Ugly biddy.

The Tillman Story — Pat.

....

I'm Still Here — Joaquin' off.

Machete — Mex pain.

The American — Idle.

Going the Distance — From bad to worse.

Mesrine: L'Instinct de Mort — Killer 'n' stinked.

Last Train Home — Fu Man Choo Choo.

The Winning Season — The trouble with dribbles.

Joaquin Phoenix as kinda himself in *I'm Still Here*

Easy A — Hole.

White Wedding — Mixed reception.

My Dog Tulip — Ruff trade.

Resident Evil: Afterlife — More like afterbirth.

Genius Within: The Inner Life of Glenn Gould — Gould till the last drop.

Legendary — Mutt wrestling.

Heartbreaker — French kitsch.

Hideaway — In a cool, dark place.

The Town — Shitty city bang bang.

Devil — May not care.

Emma Stone as Olive letters in *Easy A*

....

Alpha and Omega — *Alpha* bites.

Never Let Me Go — See this.

Jack Goes Boating — Row vs. wade.

Catfish — Throw it back.

The Freebie — Gratuitous.

Picture Me: A Model's Diary — Snap judgments.

The Happy Poet — Can't get much verse.

....

The Big Uneasy — Shearer idiocy.

You Again — Totaled recall.

Legend of the Guardians: The Owls of Ga'Hoole — Hoolarious.

Buried — Trasher.

You Will Meet a Tall Dark Stranger — Seer sucker.

Waiting for Superman — Craptonite.

Enter the Void — Where prohibited.

The Social Network — ROFL ticket.

Let Me In — No, out!

Case 39 — *Case* hard-on.

Hatchet II — Moldy *Hatchet*.

Freakonomics — Subspecie.

Ip Man — Ip? Switch.

Life as We Know It — In a petri dish.

My Soul to Take — Cheese splatter.

Nowhere Boy — Jack Lennon.

Wall Street: Money Never Sleeps — Doughs off.

Shia LaBeouf is mentored by the Gekko in *Wall Street: Money Never Sleeps*

Diane Lane as housewife Penny Chenery rides *Secretariat* hard

....

Secretariat — Mane drag.

It's Kind of a Funny Story — But not really.

Tamara Drewe — A short straw.

I Spit On Your Grave — Great expectorations.

Inside Job — Loot behavior.

Red — Dwarf.

Hereafter — The dead poo.

Jackass 3-D — -Bags.

Conviction — Free dumb.

....

Carlos — You don't know Jackal.

Gerrymandering — Caught mapping.

Paranormal Activity 2 — Haunt dog.

Inhale — Sucks wind.

Rising Stars — Along with my gorge.

Punching the Clown — Thwack job.

Welcome to the Rileys — Blah blah o' Riley.

Wild Target — Aimless.

Monsters — Oink.

Oh no! It's *Saw 3D*

....

Saw 3D — Buzz off.

The Girl Who Kicked the Hornet's Nest — Raised a sting.

Shake Hands with the Devil — Bring Purell.

Eichmann — Fried Reich.

Inspector Bellamy — Depardieu diligence.

Last Play at Shea — The New York Mess.

Megamind — Nevamind.

Due Date — Past due.

....

For Colored Girls — Who have considered suicide when leaving the theatre is enuf.

127 Hours — Disarming.

Fair Game — Plame-ass.

Four Lions — Terror plotz.

Client 9: The Rise and Fall of Eliot Spitzer — Erectioneering.

Skyline — ET-bitty.

Unstoppable — Or *Who'll Stop the Train.*

Morning Glory — Morning becomes a lecture.

Tiny Furniture — A dollish pain.

You Won't Miss Me — Sad, but true.

Helena From the Wedding — Marry, marry, quite contrary.

The Next Three Days — You'll regret that you bought a ticket.

Made in Dagenham — Logy strike.

White Material — Agony and ivory.

Heartless — And brainless.

Nutcracker in 3D — Sugarplum loco.

Faster — A fleet enema.

Harry Potter and the Deathly Hallows: Part 1 — At wiz end.

Voldemort, in one of his devious disguises, menaces Hermione, Ron and Harry in *Harry Potter and the Deathly Hallows: Part 1*

Flynn Ryder checks to see if Rapunzel's carpet matches her drapes in *Tangled*

Tangled — Locks and load.

Burlesque — Cher wear.

Love and Other Drugs — All of them depressants.

Queen of the Lot — A study in starlet.

The King's Speech — Stutter steps.

I Love You Phillip Morris — The penile system.

The Warrior's Way — Spar for the course.

All Good Things — Were left out of this.

Winter's Bone — Osteopathetic.

Bhutto — Rat Pak.

Barney's Version — *Barney* rubble.

The Fighter — Jabber wonky.

The Chronicles of Narnia: The Voyage of the Dawn Treader — Narnia business.

The Tempest — In a pee pot.

The Company Men — Lay off.

Somewhere — Locale anaesthetic.

Hemingway's Garden of Eden — The scum also rises.

How Do You Know — By smell.

Yogi Bear — Ursa minor.

Tron Legacy — New *Tron* bomb.

Black Swan — Swan flake.

Natalie Portman's *Black Swan* lays an egg

The Illusionist — Hot Tati.

Rabbit Hole — Mourning sickness.

Little Fockers — Mugger Fockers.

Gulliver's Travels — Staler Swift.

Country Strong — Like the smell of cow flop.

Blue Valentine — Eros in judgment.

Another Year — Feels like two.

The Way Back — One trek pony.

Biutiful — Unsiutable.

True Grit — *Grit* and bear it.

Jeff Bridges as an eye-popping Rooster Cogburn in *True Grit*

2011

The Fighter slugs it out with *The King's Speech*, *True Grit*, *Black Swan*, *Toy Story 3*, and *The Social Network* for Best Picture 2011

Academy Awards Best Picture

The King's Speech — Oscar Milde.

....

Season of the Witch — Snored and sorcery.

The Time That Remains — As I stare at my wristwatch.

The Green Hornet — Buzzworthless.

The Dilemma — De lemon.

Every Day — Routine.

The Heart Specialist — Cardiyuks arrest.

....

Burning Palms — From jerking off.

No Strings Attached — Bonk mates.

Mumbai Diaries — India inked.

Johnny Mad Dog — Distemper tantrums.

The Housemaid — Dust might.

The Woodmans — Choppy.

The Mechanic — Grease monkey.

The Rite — Stuff.

From Prada to Nada — I wouldn't be Prada this.

Scream of the Banshee — Wail watch.

Strongman — Power balls.

The Roommate — Dorm and dumber.

Sanctum — Skankdom.

Waiting for Forever — That's what it feels like.

The Other Woman — She crabs.

Frankie & Alice — *Frankie* valley.

Cold Weather — *Brrr*lesque.

Vidal Sassoon: The Movie — If you don't look good, he doesn't look good. You must look like shit.

Orgasm, Inc. — Chick clit.

Priestly Anthony Hopkins at the Hannibal lectern in *The Rite*

....

Unknown — I wish.

Certifiably Jonathan — Winters of our discontent.

Just Go With It — Just go *on* it.

The Eagle — Has landed. With a thud.

Cedar Rapids — Iowa an apology.

Poetry — Slam.

I Am Number Four — You are Number Two.

Big Mommas: Like Father, Like Son — Gramma schooled.

Vanishing on 7th Street — The Gone Show.

Even the Rain — Can't wash away this mess.

The Chaperone — Dated.

The Last Lions — Roar sewage.

Drive Angry — Rage rover.

Hall Pass — Cheat sheet.

Of Gods and Men — Do wha deity?

The Grace Card — *Grace* slick.

Everything Strange and New — Nu?

Beastly — The beast is yet to cum.

Take Me Home Tonight — I loathe the 80s.

Heartbeats — Skip.

Justin Bieber: Never Say Never — Except in this case.

Gnomeo & Juliet — *Gnome mas!*

Juliet has a slight case of Bieber Fever in *Gnomeo & Juliet*

Rango meets his reptilian match

....

Rango — Coma chameleon.

The Adjustment Bureau — Are they chiropractors?

I Saw the Devil — Kissing Santa Claus.

Uncle Boonme Who Can Recall His Past Lives — And they bore even him.

HappyThankYouMorePlease — SadSorryLessI'mBeggingYou.

Bereavement — Lamentable.

....

Old Cats — You gato be kidding.

Sons of Perdition — Damned silly.

Red Riding Hood — Dunces with wolves.

Battle: Los Angeles — Invasion of the hottie snatchers.

Jane Eyre — Brontësaurus.

Black Death — Boobonic plague.

Kill the Irishman — Green skeeves.

Elektra Luxx — Laxx.

Certified Copy — Repro man.

Monogamy — Monotony.

Harvest — A piece of crop.

The Butcher, The Chef and the Swordsman — Attention, choppers.

Limitless — One *duh* drug.

The Lincoln Lawyer — Shysterical.

Win Win — Whine whine.

Cracks — Not wise ones.

My Perestroika — Garbagev.

Honey — Sticky.

I Travel Because I Have to, I Come Back Because I Love You — I left because I hate it.

Mars Needs Moms — They offer womb and board.

....

After her, it's doubtful that *Mars Needs Moms*

Paul — Pall.

Hop — Snore Easter.

Super — Silly ass.

Source Code — Cold *Source*.

Insidious — Is hideous.

Rubber — Dookie.

Trust — Predator drone.

In a Better World — This isn't released.

Wrecked — 'em.

Queen to Play — She was rooked.

Seth Rogen *is* Paul in *Paul*

....

The Conspirator — A plotboiler.

Scream 4 — A Craven lunatic.

Cat Run — Pussy wallow.

The Four Times — Quad injury.

The Elephant in the Living Room — Trunk in the junk.

To Die Like a Man — Trannie sez.

Meet Monica Velour — Porn yesterday.

Ceremony — Down rite awful.

Your Highness — Bud knight.

Ghostface from *Scream 4* creeps up behind Abraham Lincoln in *The Conspirator*

Baby Doll from *Sucker Punch* cold-cocks a fanboy

Sucker Punch — Dumb *Punch*.

Diary of a Wimpy Kid 2: Rodrick Rules — Wuss up.

Peep Rules — Peepee rules.

Illegal — Oughta' be.

Miral — Schnabeldygook.

Potiche — Deneuve of some people!

White Irish Drinkers — Dipso facto.

Hanna — Holey *Hanna*!

Soul Surfer — *Eh* souls.

Meek's Cutoff — At the ankles.

Born to be Wild — Beastie buoys.

American: The Bill Hicks Story — Crix nix Hix pix.

Henry's Crime — Is the director named Henry?

Rio — Rotten to the macaw.

Atlas Shrugged Part 1 — Rand illusion.

Armadillo — War is Helmand.

The original Arthur christens Russell Brand, his successor, in *Arthur*

Arthur — Deadly more.

Footprints — Missteps.

Cougar Hunting — Senior wenches.

Tyler Perry's Madea's Big Happy Family — Perry pathetic.

African Cats — Shot puss.

The Greatest Movie Ever Sold — And now a turd from our sponsor.

Incendies — Ash if.

Legend of the Fist: The Return of Chen Zhen — I was expecting John Travolta.

Fast Five — Too lame blacktop.

Prom — Miss.

Hoodwinked Too! Hood vs Evil — Farter *Hood*.

WHOOPEE FOR ELEPHANTS

Robert Pattinson & Reese Witherspoon trunk-to-trunk in *Water for Elephants*

Water for Elephants — Dumbo droppings.

Dylan Dog: Dead of Night — One dog *Night*.

13 Assassins — Overkill.

Cave of Forgotten Dreams — Au bon paint.

Something Borrowed — Like gonorrhea.

Jumping the Broom — Sickly sweep.

Caterpillar — Crawls.

. . . .

Thor — Thunder-achiever.

The Beaver — I would chuck if I could chuck.

Last Night — Low fidelity.

Hobo With a Shotgun — Tramp steamer.

Harvest — Weed 'em and reap.

Daydream Nation — I imagined I was watching a decent movie.

An Invisible Sign — No, you can see my middle finger.

Thor gets hammered

There Be Dragons — There be draggin'.

L'Amour Fou — Heave Saint-Laurent.

Priest — A clerical error.

Hesher — Metalheadache.

Everything Must Go — Ill-disposed.

Skateland — Dead rinker.

True Legend — Feud Manchu.

The First Grader — Wrote this.

Go For It! — With a knife.

Bridesmaids — A three-skanky affair.

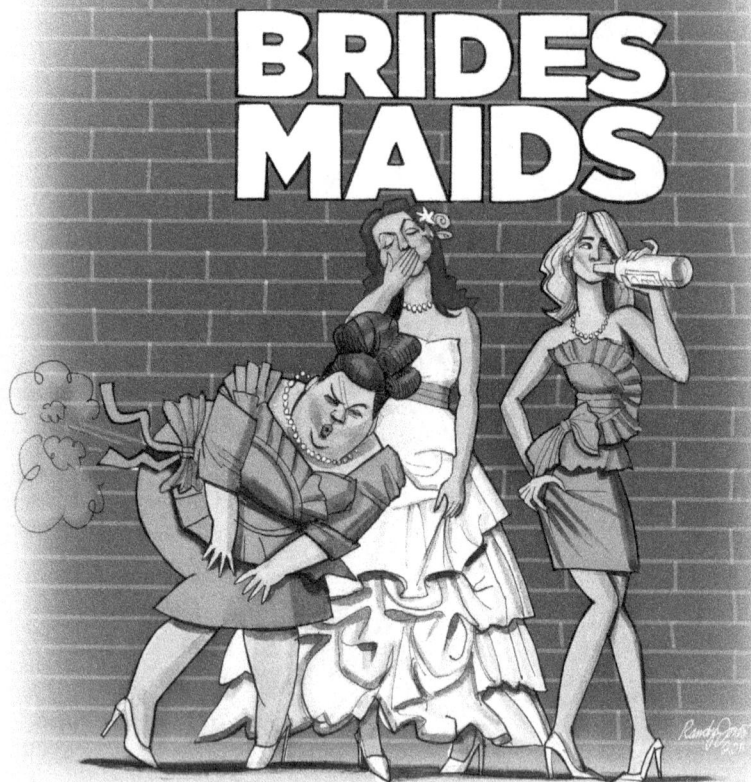

Melissa McCarthy, Maya Rudolph & Kristen Wiig party like the boys in *Bridesmaids*

Pirates of the Caribbean: On Stranger Tides — Low *Tides*.

Midnight in Paris — Clichés longue.

The Lion of Judah — *Judah* mawkish be.

We Are the Night — Total suckfest.

Bloodworth — Krisp Kristofferson.

Louder Than a Bomb — But still a bomb.

35 and Ticking — Me off.

Brother's Justice — Tae kwon dope.

The Big Bang — Whimpersnapper.

Johnny Depp's Jack Sparrow runs through the only Captain more one-dimensional than himself in *Pirates of the Caribbean: On Stranger Tides*

....

The Hangover Part II — Heir of the dog that bit.

Kung Fu Panda 2 — Po relations.

The Tree of Life — Branch rickety.

Yellowbrickroad — Where Toto peed.

Tuesday, After Christmas — When the eggnog has soured.

TrollHunter — Look on foxnews.com.

Beautiful Boy — Student bodies.

Ed Helms as Stu goes Asian in *The Hangover 2*

Wolverine, Nightcrawler, Mystique, Magneto, and Charles Xavier try to pay attention in *X-Men: First Class*

....

X-Men: First Class — Mutant strain.

Submarine — Baffles.

Beginners — Poof Daddy.

Mr. Nice — Hash mark.

Super 8 — Sprocket man.

Judy Moody and the NOT Bummer Summer — This will just ruin the first month.

The Trip — Road to nowhere.

Road to Nowhere — They made it.

....

Bride Flight — Flee-brained.

One Lucky Elephant — His part was cut.

Green Lantern — None too bright.

Mr. Popper's Penguins — Tuxedo junk. Shun.

The Art of Getting By — Mutt skills.

Kidnapped — We all napped.

My Afternoons With Margueritte — It takes a village idiot.

Buck — Shot.

R — U kidding?

Page One: Inside The New York Times — Grey Lady down.

Bad Teacher — Ed grimly.

Conan O'Brien Can't Stop — Annoying me.

A Better Life — Better than what?

Leap Year — Anus horribilis.

The Best and the Brightest — Sat this one out.

If a Tree Falls — Why can't it be on this theatre?

Farmageddon — Apocalypse cow.

....

Turtle: The Incredible Journey — Shell schlock.

Larry Crowne — *Crowne* moldy.

Transformers: Dark of the Moon — Bay at the *Moon*.

The Perfect Host — For a parasite.

Terri — Dissin' *Terri*.

Delhi Belly — Curry hurry.

Crime After Crime — On the rerun.

Cars 2 — Bumper crap.

....

Owen Wilson as Lightning McQueen and Larry the Cable Guy as Mater in *Cars 2*

Zookeeper — Ragin' cagin'.

The Ward — Cleaver.

Ironclad — Ironclod.

Project Nim — Num.

The Ledge — Jump!

The Sleeping Beauty — Sleepy. Hollow.

The Chameleon — Loose change.

Winnie the Pooh — Hunny doo.

Tabloid — On the rag.

....

The Tree — A trunkqualizer.

Gunless — Spacy heater.

The Undefeated — Palindrone.

Captain America — Panty shield.

Friends With Benefits — Perk grinds.

Life in a Day — Cam a lot.

Another Earth — Dupes.

World on a Wire — Fassblunder.

In the Company of Rohmer — A Rohmer therapy.

Horrible Bosses — Honcho notorious.

....

Kevin Spacey, Jennifer Aniston, and the genuine article in *Horrible Bosses*

Voldemort & Harry sweep up the pieces in *Harry Potter and the Deathly Hallows: Part 2*

....

Harry Potter and the Deathly Hallows: Part 2 — All Hallows heave.

Autoerotic — Rub-a-dum-dum.

The Future — Looks dim.

Cowboys and Aliens — Giddy yuck.

The Smurfs — Blue cheese.

Crazy, Stupid, Love — Crazy. Stupid. Don't love.

Sleep Furiously — I did fidget some as I napped in my seat.

....

Attack the Block — Street whacker.

The Guard — *Guard*-awful

The Devil's Double — Howdy Uday.

Spiderhole — Move over, Saddam.

Point Blank — Right, there's no point.

The Interrupters — Butt out.

True Adolescents — Bumblecore.

Without Men — Homo evictus.

Caesar gives James Franco a terrifying glimpse into the future in *Rise of the Planet of the Apes*

Jesse Eisenberg has a bomb strapped to his chest as Aziz Ansari & Danny McBride look on in *30 Minutes or Less*

Rise of the Planet of the Apes — The Tea Party gets its origin story.

The Change-Up — Low and outside.

The Whistleblower — That's not a whistle.

Bellflower — Flame retardant.

The Perfect Age of Rock 'n' Roll — Band on the runt.

Magic Trip — Bury Pranksters.

Cold Fish — On ice and it's still rotten.

....

30 Minutes or Less – Of this might have been bearable.

The Help — Less.

Final Destination 5 — Splatte finish.

Summer Pasture — Full of shit.

Glee: The 3D Concert Movie — Stank *Glee*.

The Last Circus — Insane clown pussy.

One Day — They'll stop making movies like this.

Over Your Cities Grass Will Grow — Weed be sorry.

Helen Mirren hears another great thespian emote over *The Debt*

The Debt — Tab hunter.

Conan The Barbarian — Cromcom.

Fright Night — A scareless error.

Grave Encounters — A dirt nap.

Spy Kids: All the Time in the World in 4D — 4D lashes.

Flypaper — Sticky notes.

Bad Posture — *Urggh*onomics.

Programming the Nation? — Adverts effect.

Our Idiot Brother — Leery of relativity.

Don't Be Afraid of the Dark — Dim scum.

Colombiana — Bogatard.

Brighton Rock — Grim Greene.

Circumstance — Beyond the director's control.

Higher Ground — Spirit gump.

The Family Tree — Leaf it be.

Swinging With the Finkels — Swap meat.

Apollo 18 — Drudge crater.

Shark Night 3D — Bait to the bone.

A Good Old Fashioned Orgy — Of clichés.

Love Crime — Indecent exposure…of film.

Gainsbourg: A Heroic Life — Recording with that voice did take nerve.

Hellraiser: Revelations — 1) This is the 8th sequel. 2) *The 8th sequel!*

Contagion — Bug a boo!

Warrior — Fight cluck.

Bucky Larson: Born to Be a Star — A white dwarf.

Creature — Featureless.

Burke & Hare — Doing what comes snatcherly.

Shaolin — Temple grindin'.

....

Brooks goes bumper-to-bumper with Gosling in *Drive*

Drive — Chevy chase.

Kevin Hart: Laugh At My Pain — Instead of your jokes?

Tanner Hall — Bored in school.

The Black Power Mixtape 1967-1975 — Bad Day At Black Crock.

Straw Dogs — Rape expectations.

Brother's Justice — Dax all, folks.

Autobiography of Nicolae Ceausescu — A Romaniac.

50/50 — Chemo sobby.

Bobby Fischer Against the World — The Fischer kink.

Main Street — Dead end.

Pearl Jam Twenty — Fruity preserves.

I Don't Know How She Does It — Bennies.

Restless — Lag syndrome.

Stay Cool — Drop dead.

3 — Ménage à twaddle.

Jane's Journey — Goodall girl.

Happy, Happy — A not, not joke.

Seth Rogen is half-hearted about Joseph Gordon-Leavitt's half-assed haircut in *50/50*

Real Steel — Metal punch.

The Mill and the Cross — A Bruegel shower.

Moneyball — Beane balls.

Abduction — Don't get carried away.

Killer Elite — Hit parade.

Dolphin Tale — Finny or die.

Machine Gun Preacher — Pastor ammunition.

Hugh Jackman spars with a bantam bot in *Real Steel*

The Dead — See skulls.

Dream House — A tenancy towards depression.

What's Your Number? — 0.

The Ides of March — Garbage stump.

Intruders — Trespass up.

Dirty Girl — Skanky panky.

....

The Way — No *Way*.

The Human Centipede 2 (Full Sequence) — Segmental case.

The Big Year — Trill bits.

Footloose — Cut loose…and let sink.

The Thing — Amaboob.

The Skin I Live In — Flesh in the pan.

The Woman — A dame shame.

....

Antonio Banderas "playing the fiddle" as *Puss in Boots*

Puss in Boots — Fur naught.

Father of Invention — Patently absurd.

The Three Musketeers — Sabre toot.

Paranormal Activity 3 — Ghost to extremes.

Johnny English Reborn — *English* lather.

Martha Marcy May Marlene — M-barrassing.

Tower Heist — *Tower* of bobble.

Oranges and Sunshine — Scumkist.

Taylor Lautner is stake bearer at Kristen Stewart's & Robert Pattinson's vampiric wedding in *Twilight Saga: Breaking Dawn - Part 1*

....

Twilight Saga: Breaking Dawn - Part 1 — Breaking down.

Being Elmo: A Puppeteer's Journey — Didn't tickle me.

Five Star Day — No star movie.

Margin Call — Schlock exchange.

Fireflies in the Garden — A glow blow.

The Rum Diary — Deppraved.

In Time — I will forget the anguish of sitting through this.

Anonymous — Breaking Bard.

....

Eames: The Architect and the Painter — Dead Eames.

A Very Harold & Kumar Christmas — *Harold* and mud.

Killing Bono — U2 racket.

The Son of No One — Except a bitch.

Young Goethe In Love — You Goethe be kidding.

J. Edgar — Hoover damned.

Immortals — Endless.

Jack and Jill — *Jack* 'n' off.

Melancholia — Just sad.

London Boulevard — Flush mob.

Into the Abyss — Abysmal.

The Descendants — Hawaiian paunch.

Happy Feet Two — Black and white and rot all over.

Tyrannosaur — Emotional Rex.

Hugo — Because I won't.

Arthur Christmas — Noel child left behind.

A Dangerous Method — Jung and the restless.

My Week with Marilyn — Don't bother to knock.

The Artist — Formerly known as Mince.

Rampart — LAPDatrics.

....

Walter, the newest Muppet, manipulates co-star Amy Adams in *The Muppets*

The Muppets — Rags to rags.

Sleeping Beauty — This won't wake her up.

Outrage — Tokyo woes.

A Warrior's Heart — Wasn't in it.

Young Adult — Younger dolt.

W.E. — Wee.

The Sitter — Add an H.

New Year's Eve — Auld lang swine.

Tinker Tailor Soldier Spy — Smiley entertaining.

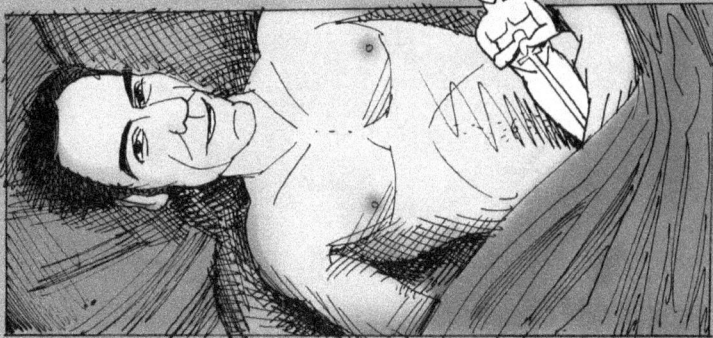

Michael Fassbender of *Shame* hopes to "polish his Oscar"

....

Shame — Sex and the shitty.

Coriolanus — Gory, all anus.

I Melt With You — Gooey.

Golf in the Kingdom — Par for the coarse.

We Need to Talk About Kevin — Son of a gun.

Knuckle — Down.

Mission: Impossible - Ghost Protocol — MI surprised?

Sherlock Holmes: A Game of Shadows — Holmes a ways from Holmes.

....

Alvin and the Chipmunks: Chipwrecked — Chip and dull.

Carnage — Feud for thought.

Satan Hates You — I admire his taste.

Corman's World: Exploits of a Hollywood Rebel — Roger & *meh*.

Cook County — Meth hysteria.

Watching TV With the Red Chinese — The Mickey Maoist Club.

Addiction Incorporated — Ciggy stardust.

The Girl With the Dragon Tattoo — Swede revenge.

War Horse — Saddle snores.

Extremely Loud & Incredibly Close — & Amazingly Twee.

Albert Nobbs — Has no knob.

We Bought a Zoo — *Bought* stiff.

The Darkest Hour — Is right before the dung.

In the Land of Blood and Honey — Jolie pit.

....

The Lady — Suu Kyi yucky.

Don 2 — Indian scummer.

The Other F Word — Flaccid.

The Reunion — Never comes together.

Pina — Bausch & lame.

The Adventures of Tintin — Wring *Tintin*.

....

Tintin hot on Snowy's heels in *The Adventures of Tintin*

2012

The Help, The Iron Lady, War Horse, The Descendants, The Artist, and *Hugo* all compete in the 2012 Oscars marathon

Academy Awards Best Picture

The Artist — Oscar mire.

....

The Devil Inside — The Exhausist.

Norwegian Wood — Not.

Beneath the Darkness — Is an ocean of dimness.

A Separation — From reality.

John Mellencamp: It's About You — Jack and dyin'.

Chico & Rita — *Chico* and the mange.

....

Contraband — Bootleg licker.

Joyful Noise — Of a whoopie cushion.

The Divide — Split peace.

Sing Your Song — *Day-o* the dead.

Man on a Mission — Waste of space.

Don't Go in the Woods — Use the port-a-potty.

Streep's steely Thatcher in *The Iron Lady*

The Iron Lady — Number 10 Downing Streep.

Lula: Son of Brazil — Hi-yo da Silva!

Albatross — It just hangs there.

Underworld Awakening — Fangs, but no thanks.

Haywire — Oh MMA God!

Red Tails — *Tails* from the cribbed.

The Red Machine — Nippon ring.

Ultrasuede: In Search of Halston — Fabriculous!

Beauty and the Beast 3D — Belle of the balls.

Belle is shown how "the Beast" really pops in the retooled *Beauty and the Beast 3D*

Carol Channing: Larger Than Life — Channing tedium.

After Fall, Winter — After film, vomit.

Crazy Horse — Cul de sex.

One for the Money — Two for the shrew.

The Grey — Poop on.

Man on a Ledge — Silly.

The Wicker Tree — *Wicker*leaks.

Big Miracle — Blubbery.

....

Chronicle — Super Fluous.

The Inn Keepers — Bed and bored.

Five Time Champion — In pocket pinball.

Windfall — Gust-busting.

Splinters — The sliver surfer.

Journey 2: The Mysterious Island — Hey, Verne, it's earnest!

The Vow — Swear off.

Safe House — Refugeniks.

....

The Woman in Black — Ghost nowhere.

Star Wars: Episode I - The Phantom Menace in 3D — Jar Jar boinks.

In Darkness — Murky murk.

Kill List — Listless.

Ghost Rider: Spirit of Vengeance — Frail blazer.

This Means War — Offensive.

The Secret World of Arrietty — Midget erasers.

Radcliffe visited by an apparition in *The Woman in Black*

Tyler Perry's Good Deeds — Do not include this.

Bullhead — Roid blunt.

Putin's Kiss — Vladdy gaga.

Deep in the Heart — Ventricle down theory.

Dorothy and the Witches of Oz — A total Baum.

Thin Ice — Frigid dare.

Act of Valor — Naivety SEALs.

Wanderlust — Rudd rover.

Project X — Degeneration *X*.

Tim and Eric's Billion Dollar Movie — Bil barely.

Gone — And forgotten.

The Lorax — Seuss and desist.

Tyler Perry tries to escape his cross-dressing past in *Good Deeds*

Danny DeVito screeches to a stop as *The Lorax*

Taylor-Kitschy-koo: Thark Tars Tarkas' tickle attack on *John Carter*

....

John Carter — Martian loser king.

Being Flynn — De Niro fiddled.

Let the Bullets Fly — Sluggish.

The Salt of Life — Grain drain.

Black Butterflies — Flutter nutter.

A Thousand Words — What this picture is not worth.

....

Silent House — Except for the snores in the back row.

Friends With Kids — Breed contempt.

Footnote — Asterisk management.

Seeking Justice — *Nyuk* Cage.

Salmon Fishing in the Yemen — Sheikh your buoy.

Jiro Dreams of Sushi — A cold fish.

The Decoy Bride — Deke head.

Jennifer Lawrence as Katniss Everdeen with her Mockingjay symbol of rebellion in *The Hunger Games*

The Hunger Games — From hunger.

21 Jump Street — Yellow school bust.

Casa De Mi Padre — *Casa* blanker.

Jeff, Who Lives at Home — Jeff bitches.

Detachment — Break it off.

The Kid With a Bike — The wheels come off.

Delicacy — Unpalatable.

Natural Selection — Survival of the shit test.

The Raid: Redemption — Kills bums dead.

The Deep Blue Sea — Kitschy sink drama.

October Baby — Prole-life.

All In: The Poker Movie — Douches wild.

4:44 Last Day on Earth — The finishing tush.

The Island President — Mal dives.

Mirror Mirror — Who's the feyest of them all?

Wrath of the Titans — Clashless.

Goon — Squat.

Bully — Wooly.

Intruders — Keep out!

Womb — Cervix.

Turn Me On, Dammit! — Turn it off, dammit!

I Kissed a Vampire — Blunder buss.

The Hunter — And pecker.

Titanic (in 3D) — Cameronic.

....

American Reunion — Banana creamed pie.

ATM — Overdrawn.

Damsels in Distress — Babes in *Doyl*land.

The Assault — On my senses.

We Have a Pope — Pope-a-dope.

God Save My Shoes — Pump and circumstance.

A Cabin in the Woods — Woody haze.

Lockout — And throw away the key.

Bad Ass — Bad everything.

Woman Thou Art Loosed: On the 7th Day — Loosers.

Wrath of the Titans' Chimera worms its way into the success of Julia Roberts' *Mirror Mirror*

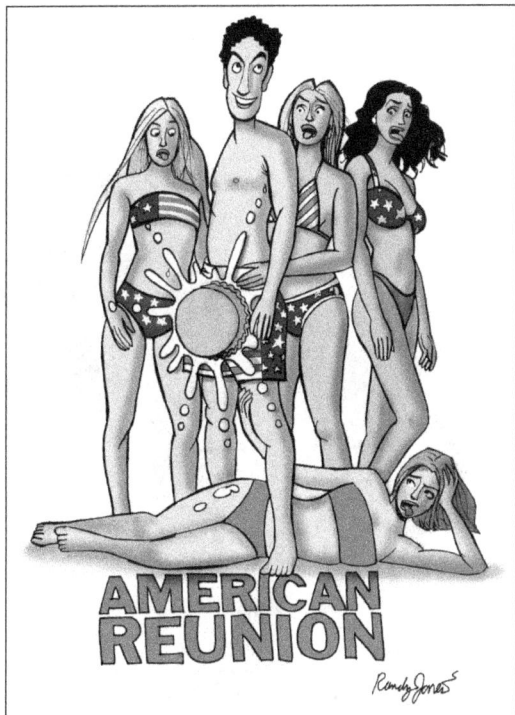

Jason Biggs impresses the babes all over again in *American Reunion*

The Lady — Burma save.

Detention — Deficit disorder.

Blue Like Jazz — *Jazz* like blew.

Monsieur Lazhar — *Lazhar* pointer.

Touchback — Worth two points.

Here — There and nowhere.

L!fe Happens — Sh!t, too.

Late Bloomers — Grey anatomy.

....

The Lucky One — Missed this.

Chimpanzee — Ape mongers.

Think Like a Man — Dumbo sapiens.

Marley — The big bong theory.

The Moth Diaries — Pupa scoop.

The Eye of the Storm — Becalmed.

To the Arctic — The polar excess.

The Three Stooges — A Fine mess.

....

Faux Stooges go back-to-back with the originals in *The Three Stooges*

The Raven — A Poe excuse for a movie.

Darling Companion — Dear in the headlights.

Zombie Dawn — Zombie yawn.

Goodbye First Love — *Oy revoir!*

Safe — Cracked.

The Five-Year Engagement — Service delays.

The Pirates! Band of Misfits — The bucs stop here.

Bernie — Weak end at *Bernie.*

Headhunters — Check up their asses.

Cusack's Edgar Allen Poe beset by *The Raven*

....

Mother's Day — Better dead than bred.

Girl in Progress — Sham Mendes.

The Avengers — Assembly required.

....

Iran Man, Hulk, and Hawkeye join forces in *The Avengers*

The Best Exotic Marigold Hotel — Imagine the *worst*.

Memorial Day — Forget this stiff.

LOL — Losing out loud.

A Little Bit of of Heaven — An itsy-bitsy bit.

Dark Shadows — The kiss of Depp.

Johnny Depp and Tim Burton unearth and abuse Jonathan Frid for *Dark Shadows*

The Dictator — Such a barren Cohen.

Meeting Evil — Hell 'lo.

The Perfect Family — Serial bomb.

Jesus Henry Christ — Cutsie roles.

God Bless America — And damn this film.

Hick — Drop the H.

Where Do We Go Now? — The discount bin.

Tonight You're Mine — Off the cuffed.

The Cup — Of gruel.

The Road — Path over.

Bonsai — Stunted growth.

Another Sacha Baron Cohen bonehead in *The Dictator*

....

Nobody Else But You — Singularly stupid.

Battleship — Alien fisher.

What to Expect When You're Expecting — This to bite.

Hysteria — Dil*doh!*

Elena — Crimea and punishment.

Virginia — Ham.

Never Stand Still — Antsy depressant.

Polisse — Brutality.

Mansome — Junk male.

Men in Black III — J, K growling.

Moonrise Kingdom — Boy scout's cookie.

Chernobyl Diaries — *Nyuk*lear disaster.

Android David seeks out his Creator in *Prometheus*

....

Prometheus — Godsmacked.

Battle Royale 3D — A *Royale* pain.

The Intouchables — Spinal pap.

Snow White and the Huntsman — Dwarful.

Piranha 3DD — 4FF.

High School — Promcom.

Hide Away — From view.

For Greater Glory — Rent a Pauly Shore movie.

Apartment 143 — Low rent.

....

The Loved Ones — Sneer torture.

5 Broken Cameras — Except the one that would've helped.

Battlefield America — See urchins.

A Cat in Paris — *Chat* on the rug.

Pink Ribbons, Inc. — Charity bawl.

Sexual Chronicles of a French Family — *Eww-la-la*.

Rock of Ages — Metal fatigue.

....

Baldwin and Brand check out Cruise's gnarly tattoos in *Rock of Ages*

Andrew Garfield of *The Amazing Spider-Man,* spars with the old guy, Tobey McGuire

....

The Amazing Spider-Man — Web drowser.

Seeking a Friend for the End of the World — Doom buddy.

Madagascar 3: Europe's Most Wanted — Not mine.

Bel Ami – Diving *Bel.*

Safety Not Guaranteed — Time stump.

Peace, Love & Misunderstanding — What's so funny about? Nothin'.

Lola Versus — From bad to *Versus.*

....

Dark Horse — 'Night, mare.

For the Love of Money — And Mike.

That's My Boy — Pater pan.

Your Sister's Sister — Sis boom. Bah.

The Woman in the Fifth — A *Fifth* of wry.

Something from Nothing: The Art of Rap — Glum rappers.

The Tortured — *aka* the Audience.

Marina Abramovic: The Artist is Present — Regift.

Abraham Lincoln: Vampire Hunter — The decapitation proclamation.

Take This Waltz — And shove it.

Brave — Fart.

Magic Mike — Privates' Benjamins.

To Rome with Love — A foul-a Roma.

The Last Ride — Rank Williams.

China Heavyweight — Oneton soup.

Grassroots — A groundsmell.

Bro' — 'Ken.

The Invisible War — The transparent trap.

Katy Perry: Part of Me — Rack Perry.

Ted — Bear, naked ladies.

People Like Us — But I don't.

Madea's Witness Protection — If you witness this, you'll need protection.

....

Ice Age: Continental Drift — Glacial stereotypes.

Beasts of the Southern Wild — New Orleans jazz.

Savages — Dealing with stress.

The Magic of Belle Isle — Isle pass.

The Pact — *Pact* rats.

Crazy Eyes — Like Marty Feldman's.

The Do-Deca-Pentathlon — O, limp pic!

Prehistoric squirrel Scrat tries to protect his precious nuts from a flying predator in *Ice Age: Continental Drift*

Batman resists the terrorist credo of the villainous Bain in *The Dark Knight Rises*

....

The Dark Knight Rises — To the level of mediocrity.

Collabrator — The puddy system.

Last Ride — You go weaving.

United in Anger: A History of ACT UP — First AIDS squad.

Red Lights — On the blink.

The Imposter — Sub human.

Trishna — Hairy *Trishna*.

Farewell, My Queen — Let them eat c**t.

....

Alps — *Oolps!*

The Runway — Hard landing.

Hara-Kiri: Death of a Samurai — Slice and dies.

The Well Digger's Daughter — Deep doo-doo.

The Queen of Versailles — Vice o' *Versailles*.

30 Beats — *Beats* the meat.

The Watch — Guard damned.

Ruby Sparks — *Ruby* slipper.

Killer Joe — Mourning *Joe*.

Little White Lies — Just lies there.

Step Up Revolution — Dance crude.

Sacrifice — A small *Sacrifice*.

Klown — Question, bro.

Falling Overnight — Brain droppings.

Ai Weiwei: Never Sorry — Weiwei out.

....

Diary of a Wimpy Kid: Dog Days — Wussy cat.

360 — Fool circle.

Celeste and Jesse Forever — Divorce case scenario.

Craigslist Joe — Listless.

The Babymakers — Screwed.

Assassin's Bullet — Blankety-blank.

Total Recall — Total reek hole.

....

Total Recall's Colin Farrell totally recalls the boob who originally played his role

The Bourne Legacy — Intelligence leak.

The Campaign — Vie?

Hope Springs — Infernal.

The Awakening — A rested development.

Red Hook Summer — Brooklyn dodgy.

2 Days in New York — Blank and white.

The Odd Life of Timothy Green — Plant parenthood.

ParaNorman — Smells like tween spirit.

....

Sparkle — Glint remover.

Cosmopolis — *Cosmo* crammer.

Premium Rush — Bike-curious.

The Apparition — Things that go bum in the night.

Why Stop Now? — I haven't puked yet.

Hit & Run — Roadkill.

Robot and Frank — Tin-skinned.

Lawless — Prohibition error.

The Expendables 2 — Sly and the Family Stone Age.

....

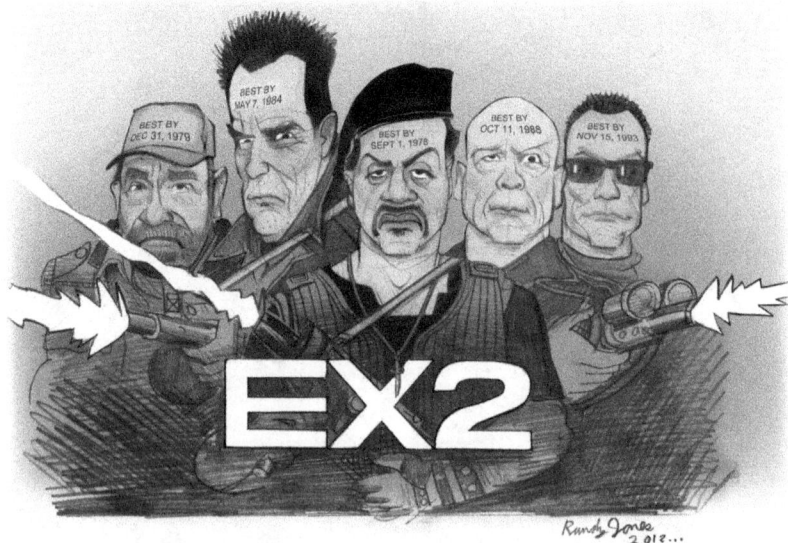

Chuck Norris, Arnold Schwarzenegger, Sylvester Stallone, Bruce Willis, and Jean-Claude Van Damme exceed their expiration dates in *The Expendables 2*

www.ingramcontent.com/pod-product-compliance
Lightning Source LLC
Chambersburg PA
CBHW031601040426
42452CB00006B/376